WHITE WOLF
SURVIVAL

BY RAY "*THE WHITE WOLF*" FRYLING

Purple Rose Ink Publications

ISBN-13: 978-1540389756
ISBN-10: 1540389758

FORWARD

Each of you reading this knows something that I do not. This brings the question, why read this book? What value does it hold for me? Why spend the time reading what I have to say?

The answer is not simple or easy, very few things in life are. But the answer is fairly strait forward: I have a lifetime of experience and the wisdom gained from those experiences. That I just survived the past thirty six years despite everything is saying a lot.

I have lived, worked, played, fought, fucked, and broken a law (or three), in thirteen countries spanning three continents—as well as in forty seven of the fifty states in The United States. In all those years, I have been able to count on less than five people to have my back long term. I learned to survive and, sometimes, even thrive. I have the scares outside and on the inside to prove it.

I have started businesses and run them—and I have shut them down when they no longer served my needs. Two of them, grossed over a hundred grand annually.

Most of the time my kids still like me, and most of the time I am on good terms with my ex-wife. So far I have never had a run-in with the law enforcement of any state or country. This is what makes me qualified to write about survival.

Why did I create the idea of Wolf Clan and why did I write about it? The answer is simple. When you cut out all the bull shit and get down to the core, where most of us prefer not to go, we all have a very basic NEED to belong. We need to know where we are accepted for who we are. We need to know who we are with, who is with us and who gives a shit about us. Essentially we all, Need to know, that someone somewhere cares. We need to have someone that we can turn to for advice. We need to know that there is someone we can turn to for help. We need to know that there is someone to turn to for an extra hundred bucks and sometimes we need to know that someone will help us get vengeance. We need to know that there is someone who will NEVER turn their back on us. That no matter what, someone will stand with us. We need to know that no matter what, no matter where we go, no matter what we say and no matter what we do that we are not ALONE.

As long as there are two people left standing the Wolf Clan is alive and YOU ARE NOT ALONE! It is the absolute certainty of this that gives us the confidence to advance, mentally, physically, emotionally, spiritually and financially. It also allows us to give to our children a future, with the possibility of power and profit.

We are Wolf Clan by CHOICE, by Blood and by our oath! Wolf Clan NEVER STANDS ALONE. We are a pack—we are family.

This is the basic of Wolf Clan Law: No one stands alone. I am the White Wolf. As long as I am alive no one in the Wolf Clan will stand alone. They can if they want to, but they won't have to. I have been many things over the years: soldier, law breaker, business man, husband and father, and political advocate. Now I am adding writer and founder of the Wolf Clan to my resume. My life is dedicated to my children and to Wolf Clan Family, and to their survival and success. I am always available to give advice. I am ever ready, to render assistance—ready willing and able to defend and where necessary avenge.

Everything I know, and every resource I have or can acquire is ready to be used for this purpose. I am not however perfect. There will be times that you will feel like I let you down, and sometimes I will. And times when I either didn't tell you or even flat out lied to you. Sometimes I will hurt your feelings but every time I do it is because in my judgment it is NECESSARY. It is not out of spite or meanness. I can and do make mistakes. Everyone does!

There will be times when a command decision is needed. Time and circumstances permitting, I will gather input, from Wolf Clan members. At times that will not be possible and I will make the decision. Because I am not perfect sometimes it will be wrong and when that becomes apparent I will correct it.

The choice to be Wolf Clan is permanent. We don't do take backs or do-overs. Make no mistake—becoming Wolf Clan is a "CHOICE" that each makes for themselves. It cannot and must not be made without a full understanding.

Teaching those that Choose to Be Wolf Clan the life skills that are needed to survive and to thrive in any environment and in any situation, is one of the most honorable and critical tasks a man can do with his life. Living up to the task is hard—maybe even impossible. But each of us needs to make the attempt.

To teach survival skills you must first know them, and practice them in your daily life. Only then can we demonstrate that we are competent teachers.

WOLF CLAN CODE

The first thing to recognize is that there are only four kinds of people in the world that we will encounter in our everyday life. And that every person you encounter is either a Predator or they are the Prey. Family/Wolf Clan can be either. The trick is knowing which you are and acting accordingly.

The following are the four basic types of people:

Family/Wolf Clan

Friends/Valued Associates

Enemies

And everyone else who has not yet demonstrated which of 1-3 they are.

When we first meet a person, we do an instant evaluation of them. This first impression is rarely completely accurate. But it is a start. Our goal is to surround ourselves with family/wolf clan, and with friends and valued associates. This takes time and effort and requires that we understand each of the four types of people.

The first thing to understand is that there are two types of family. There is the family we are born into, and then there are those that we choose, i.e., Wolf Clan. The family we are born to are not always worth the oxygen that they consume. The family that we choose is our true family. They are the ones that have demonstrated that we can trust them to have our back no matter what. If we are truly lucky, some members of the blood family are also Wolf Clan. This is not always the case though. True Wolf Clan members have made an unstated and unwritten oath to themselves to have their brothers and sisters back: right, wrong, legal or illegal. They have your back no matter what.

The modern media has given the term "Predator" a bad name. It is my belief that there are two types of predators. There is the kind that will protect, provide for and generally take care of those that belong to them. These are what I call Alpha's. And then there is the type that, fast or slow, uses up those that belong to them, and then discards them as no longer being of use. Those of us that belong to

Wolf Clan are the first kind. We do not tolerate the second kind in our inner circle. To belong to the Wolf Clan a person does not need to be a predator. Those that look to us for protection, guidance, defense and vengeance are also part of our clan/family. We Predators take care of our own. If someone harms one of ours there will be consequences, appropriate consequences, regardless of what the "Law" says.

The knights followed a code. That code said; if they look to me for protection you better not fuck with them. They are mine. That loyalty ran both ways. This is true of Wolf Clan. It is the Noble Obligation. A man of honor, aka Wolf Clan, is a valuable member of society, even though society does not recognize him as such. And Wolf Clan does not give a shit for society's approval. Wolf Clan members are what we are (Predators and Protectors).

The Predators that use those that belong to them up, and cast them aside should take care **not** to cross us or those we care for. We have all seen them operating: Abusive husbands and boyfriends, child abusers freeloaders and deadbeats. These are the predators— threats to our family and society—that give ALL predators a bad name. These are our natural enemies, and are to be removed from our daily lives at every opportunity. Removed by any means fair or foul. They will drain you emotionally and financially then cast you away. It is our responsibility, as part of the Wolf Clan, to protect ourselves and those that look to us for protection from them. Be aware of them and take active measures, legal if possible and illegal if legal fails.

Our friends/valued associates will probably be the largest group of people that we have regular interaction with. It is in this group that we find the people that we enjoy associating with. We may enjoy hunting, fishing, camping, backyard barbequing and working beside at our job with them. We share common hobbies, likes and dislikes, or business interests. As long as we understand the limits of these friendships and do not ask more than can be expected of them, or more than they are capable of, then there is a great deal of long term satisfaction from the association.

Valued associates are those that we either work with or do business with. They conduct their business in a manner so that everyone makes a reasonable profit on each transaction that is done. These are the people that we want and need to make alliances with. And these people are to be protected almost to the same degree as Wolf Clan family members. There are too few of them in the world. Friends and valued associates is our FIRST location of choice when seeking new Wolf Clan members.

True enemies are rarely hard to find if we are paying attention. They are typically the kind of predators that give us a bad name. They can also be identified as those that have deliberately harmed us or someone under our protection. Never forgive an enemy and if they do us or one of ours harm PAYBACK IS REQUIRED to the proper degree. Enemies cannot be ignored in the hope that they will go away. They must be dealt with. And yes, I know that handling things ourselves is sometimes against the law, but that doesn't mean it's morally wrong.

Finally there is everyone else, or to put it another way, those that have not been assigned a 1-3 status. These are the people that we only encounter infrequently or not at all. Typically they are a nonissue until or unless they enter our daily orbit. The world is a cold lonely wolf eat dog world, unless we have back up. The Wolf Clan is that back up.

When looking for someone to be Wolf Clan, what do you look for? To answer that question we need to define what Wolf Clan Values are, and why we value them.

Wolf Clan Values

The Wolf Clan values courage—physical courage, moral courage and mental courage. The Wolf Clan values toughness. Because what we believe in is not always politically correct, or even legal, courage is needed to stand up for what you believe to be right. Courage is needed to do what needs to be done. Sometimes it means we get our ass kicked physically, financially or legally because sometimes we have to make the fight even when we know we are going to lose the fight. Courage is needed because everything has a price that must be paid, and sometimes we can't see the full price tag. We need courage because we will do what we believe is right regardless.

The Wolf Clan values competence. When a task is important enough to do, it is worth doing well. Take the time to improve each skill you gain. If it was important to learn it, get good at it. Learn new skills, you don't need to be expert, but you do need to gain competence. Perfection is desired, but not required.

The Wolf Clan values honesty within the clan. Honesty gives us credibility. The more painful or embarrassing it is, the greater that credibility is. On very rare occasions, when life or liberty is at stake, our credibility may be the only thing that keeps us free and wins the day. A single lie, no matter how well intentioned can destroy a lifetimes worth of credibility. Take the hit and tell the truth. Lie only with great caution and great cause. I learned this lesson the hard way.

The Wolf Clan values commitment. First, you need to be very careful what you commit yourself to. When you do commit yourself to something, follow through completely. If it turns out to have been a bad move, take your lumps and learn from you mistake. If it was a good move, enjoy your just and proper reward. Regardless, don't whine over a bad move or brag over a good one. Just keep learning and earning

These are the things that wolf clan values. This list is not all of them—just the highlights. It is up to you to add to or subtract from this list.

Wolf Clan Conduct

There are many forces in this world that are totally outside of our control. Sometimes those forces kick the shit out of us, take everything from us, and strip us down to the basics. When this happens, and it does happen, what you know is all you have left. And what you know is something that nothing and no one can take from you. Be strong mentally, physically, spiritually and financially and you cannot be defeated. You can only be slowed down. Only you can surrender, if you refuse to surrender you cannot be defeated, they can kill you but they cannot defeat you.

I have noticed that a lot of people are nicer to complete strangers than they are to those in their family and those in their inner circle of friends. Your family and friends, your valued associates and members of wolf clan actually deserve our acts of kindness. Practice random acts of kindness and encouragement among the Wolf Clan. The fact is that the stronger your bonds are, the stronger the clan is. And the stronger the clan is the better the chances are that we all survive. So, do something nice for a clan member just because.

I learned the hard way that once you say something it can NEVER be unsaid. The things that are said in the heat of the moment can and do bite us in the ass later. My advice is to practice thinking before you speak, this will cut down on the things we wish we never said. It will also make you look wise, so practice thinking before you offer an opinion or advice. Sometimes your advice will be ignored, but sometimes it will be acted on. You want it to be good advice if and when someone actually acts upon it.

One of the hardest things for me to do is to make allowances for what I see as faults in others. I sometimes forget that I have faults of my own and that others let me have them, and still like me. So forgive the faults you see in others, because you have plenty of your own that need forgiving.

At one time or another we all conduct business. It may be a job we are trying to get, or a business deal we are trying to close. Either way, what we are doing is no one's business unless they are actively involved in the deal. The old saying "loose lips sink ships," is true. Most people will tell you all about what they are doing or trying to do. Members of the Wolf Clan never talk about wolf clan business with outsiders and only those in Wolf Clan that are actively involved in the business at hand. Keep your cards close to your vest. Those that do business with us will appreciate our discretion, and will be more likely to do repeat business with us.

When the Wolf Clan does business, we always try to make a reasonable profit on every deal we do. We don't try to make a killing, just a reasonable profit. The reasoning is simple. We want repeat business and if the people we do business with discover that we are making a killing instead of a reasonable profit they will take their business to someone else. Making a killer profit causes envy and resentment, but making a reasonable profit for both parties and they will do business with you again and again.

We all have needs, and we all have wants. Knowing the difference is critically important. Each of us needs to develop the personal habit of taking care of the needs first. Then with the remainder of our time and resources we can play with a clear conscience.

In a perfect world we would never have the unfortunate situation of having an encounter with the police. Since it is an imperfect world though, it is likely that you will at some point. A few years ago, I got a security guard license. The class was taught by a sheriff's department deputy. I am paraphrasing what he said: When encountering a police officer there are four things you must do, call a lawyer, then shut up, shut up, shut the fuck up! You don't know HOW to word a statement to the police to NOT be charged with a crime, and how you word that statement is what a prosecutor uses to determine whether to charge you. You have the right to have a lawyer present during questioning. Use that right to your advantage. If, in the advent that you are engaged in questionable activities of a legal nature, have a lawyer and a plausible front. Remember, lawyer up, shut up, shut up, and shut the fuck up!

When you are faced with an obstacle or situation, pause for a moment, evaluate the situation, and remember there are no instant fixes and there are many possible fixes available. Our survival skills that we practice and become good at will give us the best path to not only survive, but to thrive in almost any situation. Once we have chosen a course of action, we can then begin taking the steps needed to fix things. Remember, take a long view. It's a marathon not a sprint, most of the time. Fix things a little at a time. After all, a one hundred sixty pound man can eat an elephant—one bite at a time. Other people can slow you down. They can make things harder for you, but only you can stop you.

Everyone wants to be lucky. My definition of good luck is simple and I believe accurate. Good luck is when proper planning meets the proper action. In my time in the army I learned that ANY action is better than NO action, even if it was not the best action. It can be said that proper planning prevents piss poor performance and when acted on leads to good luck.

Everyone wants power, and there never seems to be enough to go around. There seems to be five basic kinds of power: physical, mental, spiritual, political and financial. None of them are easy to gain, but all of them are easy to lose. And all of them make others jealous when they see that we have them and they don't. The truest power is a balance of all of them. Balance is the hardest to achieve and the easiest to lose, so gather your power carefully and quietly. Use it carefully and quietly for the benefit of yourself and the Wolf Clan and you will likely have it when you need it the most. Power is attractive; it draws people to us like bees to honey.

A major university did a study on the power of setting goals. The data suggests that people who have written goals and update them regularly out produce those that have no written goals a hundred to one. Set goals, write them down and take small regular steps toward achieving them. When you are setting your goals, don't just think about next month or next year—think long term. Think, how are these goals going to benefit my kids and grandkids? What will they gain for wolf clan in the generations to come? Doing this will generate wolf clan family power for generations to come, as well as improving your life in the here and now.

Relationships are easy to get into and often end. I believe that this is most often because lust is confused with love. Do not make the mistake of confusing them. Lust can turn into love, but it is rare that it does. Most of the time lust is just lust and not wanting to be alone. On those rare occasions when lust evolves into love, it is to be valued and protected with all appropriate action and care. Make allowances for each other, you're not perfect either. When lust leads to children, the rules change. It's not about you and your partner anymore. It's about the kids. They are the future generations of the Wolf Clan family that we are fighting for. Love the children without reservation. Give them the skills and tools that they need to make informed choices for their life. Then give them the freedom to make those choices even when you don't like them. Love them, teach them, encourage them, provide for them and protect them the best you can. And when you run short on resources, ask for help from the Wolf Clan. If we have it we give it. Never, ever let a child believe that they are not loved. When they make life choices as they grow that you don't like, shut up and let them live it. It is their life, their choice, not yours. And when they fail, pick them up and help them start again. Our children are our future and the future is theirs.

Men show your woman every day, in public and especially in private that she is important, valued, respected and loved. She is you woman. Let her know that she is valuable and that she is yours and make damn sure she knows you love her. In the bedroom she is a Goddess, worship her body, and make every effort to satisfy her each time you make love.

Women you have the Right to respect—in public, but especially in private. The flip side of that is, don't disrespect your man. To get respect you must give respect. Never accept less. The Wolf Clan will back you up on this. In the bedroom you are a Goddess to be worshipped. Make sure he gets what he wants and that so do you.

Our children are our immortality. Long after we are dead and gone, the things we teach our children live on in them and in what they teach their children. Our lessons, values and even the way we think have lasting effects on future generations. It is our responsibility to make sure that the Wolf Clan values live on in them. One of the things we encounter in Wolf Clan is one of the things that everyone encounters—the end of relationships. When these relationships involve children things get complicated, but they can remain simple in your heart and mind. A child is born into Wolf Clan and remains part of the Wolf Clan forever. The mother of that child, even if she wants nothing to do with Wolf Clan, still has the Protection of the Wolf Clan.

The Wolf Clan may stand alone if that is their wish, but they never need to. All the Wolf Clan stands ready, and willing to aid any other Wolf Clan member. No exceptions. EVER! As your skills and wisdom increase, you will modify this guide to suite yourself. This is only a guide—not a mandate. Enjoy and good luck to us all.

Wolf Clan Skills

I am a warrior. I have always been a warrior and always will be a warrior. The things which I value main stream society views with suspicion, misunderstanding and contempt. What's my response? Fuck Them! I am not writing this for them. I am writing for those of you that need to find your place to belong. I am writing for those of you that feel like you are alone. You are NOT alone. We are just few and far between. It is time for us to define our place and who we are. Most will not agree or accept the common perception and that's ok. Most people could not handle this degree of reality. The bread and circuses that they observe limits them too much.

American society as it exists in 2016 is doomed. It cannot continue in its current form for long, and when the inevitable collapse happens, the skills and mind set outlined in this booklet may make the difference between survival and death.

A fundamental skill of the survivor is knowing the difference between wants and needs, and properly allocating available resources to meet them. I have found that the majority of people confuse the two. They classify wants as needs without a second thought. This critical mistake leads to wasted resources, wasted time and a potential shortage of necessary skills and supplies on the day of reckoning.

You are your greatest resource. You also have resources of time, energy, money, and skills. The more of these you have the better your chances. Critical thinking and reasoning skills will be very valuable to you. They take practice, but you can get some books on the subject from the local library, or from the web.

The skills you need come in two broad categories, Pre-collapse and Post-collapse. Some of the skills are valuable in both arenas, and some apply to only one or the other. It is up to you to decide which one's you learn and in what order. You are the master of your destiny. I am only trying to point you in the right direction—not dictate every little thing.

Basic needs include: food, water, clothing, shelter, transportation, defense and communication. Gaining these necessities in the proper order and in a timely manner can be a neat trick that requires, at the least, a modest income. The more modest the income the better you must become at asset allocation. Most people equate income with a job, but it can also come from investments or businesses that you create for the purpose.

This brings us to the question of what are your current are and what are the skills you need to have more of. Take a minute and make a short list of everything you know how to do. This list gives you your starting point for your income generation. An example could be: mowing the grass and weed eating. A friend of mine went to the U.S. Virgin Islands and got a job weed eating for ten dollars an hour while living in a tent on the beach. This allowed him to extend his stay. He left with more money than he arrived with and had a blast. He successfully pulled off a low cost, low stress vacation with very little work. However, some of us have a hard time getting or maintaining a job. For us self-employment is the logical choice for generating an income. It can be as simple as a lawn mowing service or as complex a service or product as you can imagine. If you have an income that covers all of your wants and needs, Congratulations. Not many people ever achieve that degree of independence.

In the pre-collapse society food is one of our major expenses. It is also one where we have the greatest control and the one where most of us exercise the least control. It is possible to eat three meals a day in this country for one dollar a day, or less. I proved it to my own satisfaction by going to the Dollar General store, and making a list of foods that can be prepared on a cost per serving basis. Using that criterion, I came up with a menu of meals you can make for a dollar a day and eat three meals a day. You can eat three meals a day for three days for the cost of one value meal from a fast food restaurant. Test it for yourself. The point of this is to establish an income/outlay that leaves something to invest in additional skills and supplies for when the collapse happens. The better prepared you are the better your chances.

My recommendation is that you determine what you are going to need for a specific time period, and start gathering the food items and tools you are going to need to make it through the initial insanity. A one pound bag of dried beans will store for up to five years if it is properly sealed and it has thirteen servings in it. The cost with tax is one dollar and six cents. Boring, but it is edible and durable. If you have never had a garden it is an easy way to cut your food bill. You can grow a lot of food in a small space with a little thought, planning and effort.

There are several companies in my area that pay you every day that you work. I once supported myself for almost a year working at one of them. They don't pay a lot, but every day you take home money that can be converted into supplies and tools. A few of the additional benefits of working for them are they supply your equipment and they don't discriminate against ex-convicts or people that can't pass a drug test. If you need cash right away, they are a good place to start. Showing up to work on a regular basis and working hard can easily lead to a more permanent position.

Another source of ready cash is to donate plasma. If you are eighteen and in good health you can easily make up to two hundred a month doing this. The registration process takes about five hours and gets you forty five to fifty dollars. FYI drug testing is sometimes required as well as a background check, so it may not be for everyone.

One of my favorite small side businesses to run is lawn care for the simple fact that they are easy to start and run. Not to mention that you may already have the skills you need and all the tools you need. The down side is that they are seasonal in my area—typically April first to October thirty first. If you combine that with a work today pay today company though, you can remain gainfully earning year round. If your area has a regular supply of firewood you could augment by cutting and selling firewood two. All of these options are profitable, easy to start, and the capital investment is very small. Be your own boss.

At this time scrap metal is low. But it only takes approximately thirty six aluminum cans to make a pound, and two pounds buys approximately thirteen servings of our budget menu. Junk cars can be very profitable if you get them free in exchange for hauling them away. If you have to pay for them, you may need to separate them to get the best price for your scrap.

Last year I was able to make money picking up black walnuts for free from the city park, and selling them at the collection point for fourteen dollars a hundred pounds. Not a great fortune but welcome none the less.

The ways in which you can make money are virtually endless. Your only limitation is your imagination. Use these particular ideas as you see fit or don't use them. Mix and match or choose an altogether different approach. You are your architect, the master of your own destiny. Make your own plan, one that suites your own personal situation and get started. Take action NOW!

Food and water are two of our basic needs. If you are interested a large percentage of your food can be generated from a garden, drying, root cellaring and canning. But one source of food that should not be neglected is hunting and fishing. A Fur, Fish and Game license is cheap if you utilize it as a food source in addition to a recreational pastime. Put the deer, the turkey and the fish in the freezer instead of on the wall. The down side? I don't see one.

The final source of food is forage. It may or may not be legal to pick over a farmer's field after the harvest, but if you ask he will likely give permission. Persimmon trees grow in fence lines next to the roads and public lands. Old abandoned orchards or apple trees on vacant property are also sources of free food. Once you start looking you could be amazed at the amount of food out there that you never noticed before, and every dollar you save is a dollar available to buy supplies.

The books written covering survival tools are legion, so I will keep this part short. The Frontiersman left home and headed west with some very basic tools, and most of them doubled as weapons. Essentially they were: A rifle, a knife, a tomahawk, ammunition, a bedroll and something to start a fire with. These are the very least you should have. In addition I would add some open pollinated garden seed, and a shelter as well as some trade goods.

Your choice of weapon is a personal choice, and one that you must make for yourself and your budget. My personal choice is a 22/410 Rossi, a 22/22mag revolver and a 12 gauge. These are my choices for the following reasons: first, they are simple and second, they are effective. Not to mention, they are inexpensive to buy and so is the ammo. Your choice should fit your needs and your budget, not mine or anyone else's.

If you have time and if it is in your budget, then gather a few tools that do not require electricity. Worst case scenario, they will hold their value. Best case scenario, they save your life and the life of someone you love. Your final tool should be a first aid kit—even if it is a very simple one. You should make it as complete as you can afford, because it may very well save your life. Let's face the facts. Shit does happen! And since it happens, it is best to be prepared.

In future booklets, I will present more detailed lists of the skills and tools that I believe are and will be needed in the coming months and years. I hope and pray that I am wrong, but I will be prepared! What about you?

NOTES:_____

_____

_____

_____

_____

_____

_____

_____

_____

_____

_____

_____

_____

_____

_____